Coconut
Seed or Fruit?

By Rosie McCormick

Contents

Coconuts

Coconuts are dark brown, hard,
rough and hairy on the outside.
They have white crunchy and sweet
meat on the inside. Coconuts grow on
coconut palm trees.

Where Coconut Palms Grow

Coconut palms grow in many hot, sunny places around the world. They grow on islands and by the ocean. Many of the trees grow wild. Some are grown on large tree farms called plantations.

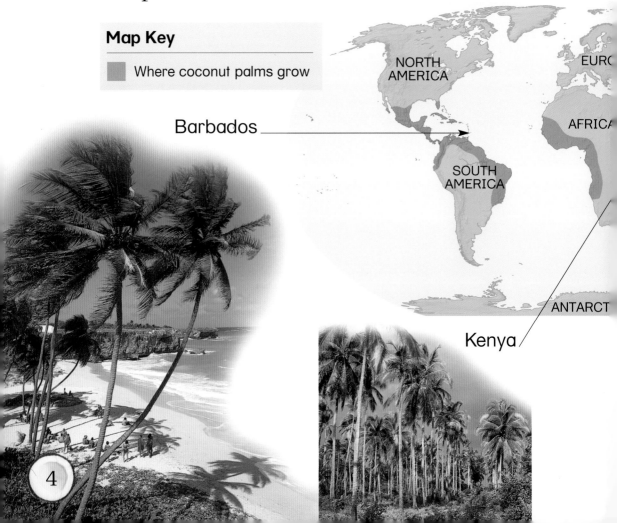

Map Key

Where coconut palms grow

NORTH AMERICA

EUR(

AFRIC/

Barbados

SOUTH AMERICA

ANTARCT

Kenya

Sometimes coconuts fall into the water. If the coconuts are washed up onto a new shore, they often grow into trees.

Coconuts float in water.

ASIA

AUSTRALIA

N
W · E
S

Fiji

How Coconut Palms Grow

Coconut palm trees are tall and thin. Some grow as high as ten-storey buildings. Their trunks are strong, but they bend with the wind. This helps keep the trees from blowing over in strong winds.

Coconut palms grow in sandy soil.
Their roots spread out far around
the tree to gather water. These roots
also hold the trees firmly in the ground.
Sometimes coconut palms
live to be one hundred
years old.

adult palm tree

leaves

coconut

leaves

coconut

young palm tree

trunk

Large green drupes grow on the coconut tree.
A drupe is a fruit that usually has one seed
inside. Coconut meat grows inside the seed.
It takes about a year for a coconut drupe
to grow.

drupe

coconut seed
inside drupe

coconut meat
inside seed

When coconut drupes are ripe, people harvest them. Sometimes people climb the trees to cut the fruit down. Sometimes they use a long pole with a knife on one end.

The coconuts we see at the market are really the seeds of the coconut palm trees. A coconut is one of the largest seeds in the world. So is a coconut a seed or a fruit? It is both.

Uses for Coconut Palms

Every part of the coconut palm tree is used.
Coconut meat in the seed is good to eat.
Young coconuts have milk to drink.

coconut milk

fresh coconut meat

dried coconut meat

Sometimes coconut meat is dried so that it lasts a long time. Dried coconut meat is called copra. People eat copra or use it to make coconut oil and coconut milk. Both of these are used in cooking. Coconut oil is used to make soap and shampoo.

coconut milk

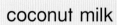

shampoo

COCONUT
Shampoo

soap

The outer shell of a coconut is called the husk. A young husk is green and smooth. An older husk is dry and brown. Sometimes the tough, stringy fibres of the brown husk are used to make mats.

coconut husk
with stringy fibres

This woman is making a mat from coconut fibres.

Palm leaves are used to make roofs and walls
on some buildings.

Coconut palm leaves are useful, too.
In some warm climates, they are used
to make roofs. They are also woven into
screens, mats and clothes.

People also use the roots and the trunk
of the coconut palm to build homes and to
make furniture.

Since all parts of the coconut palm can be used, it is a valuable tree. It has provided people with food, liquid and shelter for many, many years. In some parts of the world, this tree is an important part of life.

Index